About the Book

How are a broom, a baseball bat, a hammer, a shovel, and a seesaw alike? They all are levers. They help make work easy, and they help you move things easily or quickly.

Lisa Miller takes one of the simple machines and explains what it is, what it does, and how we use levers in everyday living, both at work and at play. Simple straightforward text and attractive illustrations that extend the text make the subject appropriate for young boys and girls beginning science.

The *Science Is What and Why* books introduce the fundamentals of science to young boys and girls. Topics of interest in elementary science classrooms are expanded and explored. These books, which have been checked for scientific accuracy by an authority, serve as excellent supplementary material.

LEVERS

lisa miller

Illustrated by
Sean Morrison

Coward, McCann & Geoghegan   New York

LEVERS

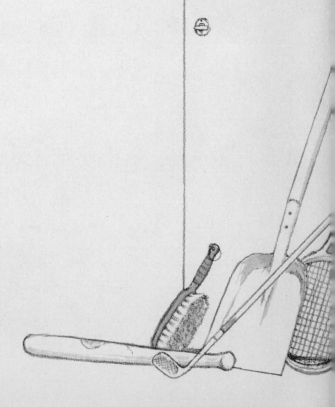

A lever makes work easy.
It helps you to move things easily or quickly.

You can lift a friend high in the air on a seesaw.

You can pull a nail out of wood with a hammer claw.

You can move a heavy rock with a broomstick.

The seesaw, the hammer and the broomstick
do not look alike but they are all levers.

Even though they do not look alike,
all levers are alike in some ways.
A lever is a bar that does not bend easily.
The bar must have a resting place.

Put a board on a log to make a seesaw.
The board is a bar that does not bend easily.
The log is its resting place.
The seesaw is a lever.

When you push the ends of the seesaw up and down,
the board turns on its resting place.
The resting place of a lever is called the *fulcrum*.

Pull a nail out of a board with a hammer claw.
The hammer is a bar that does not bend.
The hammer head on the board is the fulcrum.

Lift the end of a rock with a broomstick.
The stick is a bar that does not bend easily.
The fulcrum is the place
where the stick rests on a small stone.

The seesaw, the hammer and the broomstick are all levers.
They are all bars that rest on fulcrums.
They all help to make work easy.
Your seesaw shows you how a lever works.

Put the fulcrum right under the middle of the seesaw.
Put a big book on one end of the board.
The end of the board goes down.

When one end of the seesaw goes down,
the other end goes up.
Put your finger on the end that is up.
Push down with your finger.

When you push down with your finger,
you are using force.
The force makes the high end of the board go down
and lifts the book on the other end of the board.

When you take your finger off the board,
you take away the force.

The book goes down — BANG!

The lever helps you to lift the book
when you use force.
But when you take away the force,
the lever does not help you.

Put three big books on one end of the board.
That is a heavy *load*.
Put one hand on the high end of the board.
Can you push it down with one hand?

It takes more force to lift a heavy load than a light one.
The heavier the load, the more force you must use.

Do you think that you could lift a big dog
on the end of a seesaw?
You could if you put the fulcrum in the right place.

Try it with a friend.
Move the fulcrum so that it is near one end of the board.
Now there is a short end and a long end.

Ask a friend to sit on the short end and be the load.
When you push down on the long end of the board,
you lift your friend easily.

When the load is on the short end of the board,
a little force on the long end of the board will lift the load.

Ask your friend to sit on the long end of the board.
Push down on the short end and try to lift the load.
It is very hard to do.
When the load is on the long end,
it takes a strong force to lift the load.

A lever helps you to lift more easily
when the fulcrum is near the load.
When you change the fulcrum on a lever,
you change the amount of force that you need to lift the load.

A seesaw is a lever that helps you lift.
So is a hammer claw and a stick that moves a rock.
There is another kind of lever
that helps you move things quickly.
A fishing rod is a fast-moving lever.

On a lifting lever, you move the fulcrum
close to the end where the load is.
A fast-moving lever always has its fulcrum
farther away from the load and nearer the force end.

When you swing a fishing rod over the water,
the fulcrum is your hand at the end of the rod.
The force is your other hand.
The fishing end of the rod moves more quickly
than your hands do.

When you sweep the floor with a broom,
you are using a fast-moving lever.

A broom is one of the many levers around your house.

A pair of scissors is a *pair* of levers.
The fulcrum is the place
where the blades are joined together.
The load is the cutting end.

Where do you put the force?

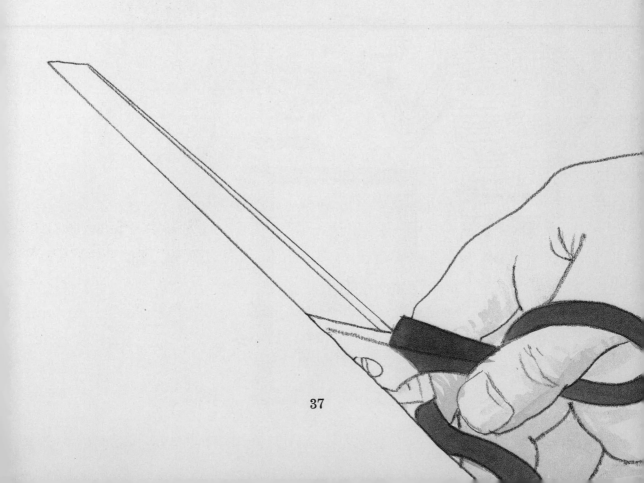

You have another lever that is all your own.
It is your arm.

Lift a heavy book.
If you bend your elbow,
the fulcrum is at your elbow.

Lift the book with your arm straight.
Now the fulcrum is at your shoulder.

Was it easier to lift the load
when the fulcrum was close to it?

You can see many levers if you look for them.
A nutcracker, a golf club, and a shovel
are a few.
Can you tell where the force, the load and the fulcrum are?
Do they help to lift things easily
or to move things quickly?

The Author

LISA MILLER lives in New York City. She attended Columbia University and after college she worked as a junior physicist for a division of the Sperry Gyroscope Company.

Miss Miller has had extensive experience in scientific research. She is the author of SOUND and WHEELS in the *Science Is What and Why* series.

The Artist

SEAN MORRISON was born in Ireland. He grew up in England and graduated from St. John's College, Cambridge. In 1959, he came to the United States where he worked as a television producer in advertising and as a film producer. He published his first book in 1963 and has been active in the children's book field ever since as editor, author and illustrator.

The *Science Is What and Why* Books

Each book in the *Science Is What and Why* series introduces fundamentals of science using a simple, attractive approach specifically designed for young boys and girls. Straightforward, lively language and distinguished illustrations which are a practical extension of the text present scientific facts as fascinating and exciting as the realm of the imagination.

LIGHT
by Bernice Kohn
Illustrated by Janina Domanska

ECHOES
by Bernice Kohn
Illustrated by Albert Pucci

SOUND
by Lisa Miller
Illustrated by Tomie de Paola

HEAT
by Howard Liss
Illustrated by Abner Graboff

ELECTRICITY
by Ben Kerner
Illustrated by Mehlli Gobhai

WHEELS
by Lisa Miller
Illustrated by Tomie de Paola

MAGNETS
by Raymond Sacks
Illustrated by Stefen Martin

TELEPHONES
by Bernice Kohn
Illustrated by Joseph Low

LEVERS
by Lisa Miller
Illustrated by Sean Morrison